VIA Folios 137

Wild Fennel

Wild Fennel

POEMS & OTHER STORIES

Marisa Frasca

BORDIGHERA PRESS

Library of Congress Control Number: 2019932508

Printed in the United States.

Published by
Bordighera Press
John D. Calandra Italian American Institute
25 West 43rd Street, 17th Floor
New York, NY 10036

VIA Folios 137
ISBN 978-1-59954-140-2

CONTENTS

I

II

III

Acknowledgments

About the Author

For immigrants everywhere

I

Life sprouts wherever it can.
—GWENDOLYN BROOKS

GATHER ROUND THE BRASS BRAZIER

When I feel a belt tightening around the chest for a hundred reasons I remember a woman who offered relief when Etna made the earth quake beneath my feet and I carried shocks and aftershocks like a second skin. After we had checked candle supplies and those with a bathtub filled it during hours of running water, Signora Garducci invited the neighborhood into her large stone kitchen. She laughed with great heaves of her gut, raised eyebrows with her stories, indistinguishable from comfort. I watched her hand throw the hard shells of almonds (after the fruit had been freed) to the brass brazier, then fan the coals, the *carbonella*. I listened to the crackle of almond shells and smelled sweet pork sausage wrapped in newspaper roasting in the coals. Signora Garducci's voice seemed to attend to all the cries of the world.

Gather round, gather round the brazier, children,
and I'll tell you a story.
Never look at the mountain without shedding a tear.
There's a god trapped underneath the mountain. His seed
of anger rises to destroy. His seed renews the soil.
The fury flows side to side and in the round of years.
We wait for the return of lost fields. In the meantime
think of Persephone who might have been scared
by Hades, that gloomy fellow, and his three-headed dogs.
The brave goddess laughed and scratched their heads.
The mulberry bush sprouted, the silkworm reappeared.
The mulberry stains everything it touches
but also improves the health of your heart.

More or less those words have stayed with me like a tender habit.

COMEDY AND TRAGEDY

Comedy and Tragedy, statues outside Vittoria's neoclassical theater, symbols of theatrical life—I stared at them every morning and afternoon while walking to and from elementary school. Apollo and his Muse and the visages of musicians, writers, Italian poets in their stone niches must have spoken to me about making art. Something like getting lost in a search larger than the self, something like your nakedness hardly belonging to you. What do those sculptures say now as I see them a second time in my mind's eye, as I dwell in ambiguity, as the heart hungers for its beauty? Longing they say because longing was long and ripe in a girl who could never run without the fuel of wonder.

The mind interrupts good tidings and flashes images of that girl wearing a smile like a borrowed dress. In America she does not speak her anguish for fear the sky may be listening, does not utter a sigh—her mother might hear the echo. She must face the inconsolable widow at the dinner table and why not translate a joke heard in English class. Maybe it will bring a moment of grace, a hint of life to her mother's eyes. And by the way, Ma, I know which bus stops near the Social Security office on Fulton Street. Don't worry, Ma. I understand English. I read and write it, can almost tell the difference between chicken and kitchen. We'll file for unemployment. I'll get a job.

The actor momentarily quelled the storm and rode the thunder. The actor remained perfectly calm and composed in her un-mendable wounds.

POEM OF EXILE

We took turns laying our heads on each other's laps.

Did we smell so much like waste?

All around us an infected spirit screamed:

detestable & unworthy

your country is sinful. Mine is full of God.

What shall I say about my friend's quivering chin,

her far-off gaze, low-tone whisper?

Neither of us could do without feeling we'd been exiled.

After pinning hours of pity on our chests

we rose from the couch,

looked out the window to find the moon.

Even she was trapped in her black cage,

& our mothers

where were they on this darkest of nights?

ODE TO WILD FENNEL
Foeniculum Vulgare

Here's to you—worshipped by the ancients
to ward off evil spirits, restore lost vision,
for treatment of poisoning & infections,
for the kisses & weeping of women
on hands & knees
or lying next to you awhile
in open fields aflame with green,
consuming the tissue that sweetens breaths,
helps breast milk flow
always the healing herb in prayer & in fever.

Here's to your caned stems & lacy fronds
old as the bird, the wind, the migrant's shoes
that dispersed your anatomy of miracles
from the Mediterranean basin
to new sea cliffs, yard shrines, cracks
in the road, gravel driveways
of stately homes, & neighborhoods
brimming with crumbling foundations.
In a world where despair & disparity grow,
wild fennel, you sneak up on us like love.

My heart swells
you still appease the poor man's hunger,
trim appetites of the rich grown too fat,
take root by the graves of the dead
where human wars are over.
I wish I could be a charitable plant
with no sense of self importance,
no clever perspectives
drinking sunlight & filaments of rain,
assisting all sentient beings in need
but I'll say no more about that.
They prescribe medication
for this kind of talk in America—where I
struggle like hell to be merciful.

I could speak a well of anger
about new wars, border walls, & how
the clock is moving
between one breath & another for all of us.

But to see you is to see
free, unending life at work.
I can touch & taste —uninterrupted
life from before there were rooftops.
What gift to find you here beside a stone
among last year's brittle oak leaves
as the April night descends
& there's a bit of wind makes you tremble,
makes a baby rabbit up its ears & pose.
Everything else is quiet in Oysterponds.
Can you see me bend & bury my face
deep into your willowy leaves?
I'm so grateful for the green elegance,
won't even close my eyes, as in prayer.
All of me wide open & wake, inhaling
sweet licorice scent
for a moment of uncomplicated happiness.

GAZZOSA

Sicily's effervescent soft drink

Like Alchemists we could turn water gold
The art of transmuting was shrouded in ritual

On that island with a thousand days of sun
Limestone hills glittering from dawn to dusk

We had spring water, cane sugar, plenty of
Juicy oranges waiting to be squeezed

Our liquid whirls in a bottle fermented in the sun
The kitchen window flung wide, & when

A sparrow came to the sill we took it as a sign
Time to shake, twist, turn upside down the vessel

Did we pop a cork? Snap a wire latch?
I know that froth rushed out like the sea

Frantic vapor hit cheeks, tickled noses
We children couldn't push back such joy

& while our delirious eyes continued to examine
Wonder! The thing that requires

The same muscle as tears, the thing that wells up
Uncontrollably. You could dance that tangle of

Emotion—like a foot-stomping routine
You could slide across the floor chanting Gazzosa

Where solemn songs of the poor also rose
& soon those sacred sounds began to stun us

Out of bubbly moor & navel oranges
Oozing out in a golden stream.

THE GOLDEN BASIN

On that fertile island dubbed *Conca D'oro*
today there's still a farmer

He falls in desperate silence
hearing things the wayward wind tells his daughter

a life outside the barn,
a life of smoother hands, an education

—a wish for something better
than wringing a poor chicken's neck

Another homestead shutter shuts in eternal winter

A farmer falls to his knees
hearing things the seductive sea tells his son

no more tilling land deprived of a spit of rain, no more
sun baking your neck like shoe leather

& what difference does it make if
the restless board planes to America, the UK

Australia, or hop on trains to Germany.
Along the way & along somewhere

none see mothers turning kitchen cupboards
into altars, how candles burn near photographs

of departed children good as dead,
how fathers raise palms of arid earth

in consolation. How citrus & olives
swollen like desire are rotting in the fields.

UNDER THE SKY OF LAMPEDUSA, 2016

Tell me little one
what name your precious mother chose to give you
was it gift
was it flower

Tell me little one
when your breasts began to bud
did your brother frown
stand firm with stick in hand to scare your suitors

Did you walk holding your father's arm
I bet he secretly smiled when young men called you beautiful

For elder faces of your desert village
were you breath of air

maybe high tower when you climbed the boat of hope
never making that last ½ mile across

Tell me little one
what name
to give these men in face masks
carrying your drowned body on a stretcher

what name
to search & rescue
tagging your blue-black ankle—#99

AMORETTO

I write your name on the sand
a loud wind spreads its wings
erases evidence of your existence

Little love, you don't see or hear
but shape the earth itself
with your form after death

CAMPANILE DI VECCHIO CURON

On rigid winter nights an old Tyrol woman
hears bells ringing from the depths of Lake Resia

Vecchio Curon

From her alpine home she can walk to that church
the spire & mildewed cross of the 14th century steeple

Stroke the tower
kneel in the middle of a frozen lake
that flooded old Curon

There are her dead lying in the basin

She waits to be consoled

Ours is not the only drowned village in the world

Vecchio Curon

Ours not the only dam or hydropower plant

Vecchio Curon

Church half-risen on man-made lake
ringing & rusting tombstone

FANTASIA

Locked in a one-on-one dance with fantasy

If he walked in now what would I say?

Stay

I'll move closer in summer robe of Queen Anne's lace

No small talk. Undo the robe

To those pleasures wheeling in my head

Candlelit & musical place

I'm infantilized with the god of wine

The singer's sweetest song holds us

The spooky bass, bluesy beat

Music & myth save us from our ugly stink

A cool forgetting   alive

Is painful business

THIS TIME

This time with a burlap knapsack full of seeds,

no toiletries, change of clothes,

just the seeds weighing as much

as I'm allowed to carry on Jet Blue.

This time I'll spill more than words on the White

House lawn, the people's lawn,

& in no time at all

the perfectly manicured, perfectly uniform

Kentucky Bluegrass will make space

for red clover & white clover

& yellow chicory flowers & mock olive

& varieties of black nightshade.

Can you see their spines rising,

necks stretching far as the Lincoln Memorial,

far as King's stone of hope. The Mall

blanketed with dazzling color.

How exquisite those menacing weeds—

MINE IS ONLY A NIGHTMARE

Since fear found me & sanity betrayed me

What's that noise?   THAT NOISE

A recurring ICE nightmare
since I began to leap out of bed
as if a shotgun were pointed at my back.
Since I became a nighthawk
running from room to room
in a desperate search for proof.
Where's my old green card?
Where my naturalization papers?
Where my kids' birth certificates from NY Hospital?

THE STILL POINT

I dreamed of Anna with wild green hair
— a giant nest.
An old spider crawled out & spoke:
"Have mercy on my soul"

Other long-gone beings—faceless
gathered under a willow,
red ivy blazed along the trunk,
spider dangled from a low branch

A lake edged with cattails shook with light
& the faceless shining in their clothes
pointed fingers at Anna whose heavy head hung:
"We're all here because—nowhere else to go"

Every being in the dream began to fall asleep
& with them the spider, the ivy faded.
The lake was still, not a leaf stirred in the tree.
Nothing more was seen

I woke in panic—didn't know who or where
I was. Only later & through the day
my mind ruminated—all dissolves
until someone remembers who we are.

APPARITION

Bare-chested boys slide-tackled, scissor-kicked soccer balls & backslapped each other. Men in flat caps talked politics & played cards by the Monument of Fallen Soldiers. There we were, Anna & I, in the Piazza del Popolo—Square of the People—that was not for all people, not respectable girls unescorted & not for the Roma, (then called Gypsies or women of the night) who carried larger burdens than ours. Anna & I ducked & crouched like thieves crossing the Piazza—to reach a houseless lot behind the church of San Giovanni. A mulberry forest grew in that forbidden spot where we spied such a woman in broad daylight. White flower in her mop of curly hair, red skirt tangled round her waist, mound of black between her legs—waiting to make some scrawny fellow feel like a magnificent horse, or so we said out loud to each other, Anna & I, wide-eyed. How impossible it was that our Gypsy arched toward sunlight was not a celebrated act of God. We named her *Beatifica*, Blessed One, in her everlasting world. But fear soon overtook our little pleasure spell & suddenly an alarm. Today I'd call it a panic attack, complete disintegration of power like hyperventilating in a crowded commuter train, turning red & pale in the face at once. One of us went weak in the knees & arms. One of us dropped the shoebox that held our *Nutella* sandwiches. I can't remember who said there must be a venomous snake in our brains, after we could speak again. We ran out of that thorny forest to someplace safe from our own deep places. Soaked in summer sweat the conversation turned to mothers—if our mothers had known how we'd thought of that woman as a holy apparition, they'd shroud us in black, drag us directly to The Sisters of These Last Days—in rehearsal for our own funerals.

THE SEWING SCHOOL

In Elvira's walled-in garden with concrete floor
was one potted plant—crown of thorns
sprouting red flowers the size of dimes

But if you looked at each student's hoop
—a dozen species of embroidered buds,
early leaves in playful grace
for linen sheets & coverlets to match

Birds waited for a second wing
to take flight in feather stitch
— nightgowns of batiste—young women
would wear once. Wedding nights

Elvira did you lose your savage cry in the throat of birds?

Elvira in black stockings through heat & cold
Elvira long, thin—a humpbacked crow
stooping over girls' trousseaus, & women
tailoring dresses for births & deaths

Everyone, everyday—seam, baste, band & stitch
& in so doing they built a history
as if those females lined up in rows
had been born into bondage of cloth.

SKIN LIKE A SERPENT

Sit like a hermit with headlamp on

Look inside your deep cave

Here & there crawl your way through the dark

Shed old insular skin like a serpent

Return to the arch as dove with olive twig

Two worlds exist to disorient & enlighten

One pushes against the other

Or have I internalized Cesare Pavese so fully

I too need a village

If only

For the pleasure of leaving it

BAUDELAIRE STAYS THE NIGHT

Baudelaire lies open on the left side of my bed
where a live man with outstretched arms should be

enjoying the view from my pied-a-terre.
I bought this box in the sky with fatiguing efforts
to climb the American social ladder,
mistook paradise for a view of the 59th Street Bridge,
stream of cars coming & going.
Symphonic hum. A crash expected any time.

Is everybody rushing to another giddy celebration
of art?
I am tired
of all the taste & aftertaste of entertainment —
no desire for well-dressed friends, after-theater-drinks,
poetic showmanship, applause.
Cities feel like fakes that postpone
how we're deceived.
                     Paris, the Far   *gris*
overblown.
Only the Frenchman beside me soothes,
explodes: "This life is a hospital where every patient
is possessed with the desire to change beds."
I want to steal his fingerprints —
touch myself like a woman while I still can,
that tender part worn thin with age,
the feel of silk. His hand my own—sweet lament.

BETWEEN THE LIONS

A homeless man sprawls his body on a step
between Patience & Fortitude outside the public library

What faith binds him to this earth? Maybe he prays
to marble lions: Help me survive a winter's night

I can tell you he buttons his tattered shirt to the neck,
pulls up his socks, a dead cigarette stuck to his lip

Now his hands embrace his knees, he's curled
on a bed of cement & blinks like a lamenting star

Store windows glisten with manikins
dressed in fur-lined hats & goose-down puffers

The stars have hidden in the heart of the city,
the moon sold out, snow falls thick, slow & silent

Two majestic lions sit without blood, scorn,
without thorns, staring blank & stone-quiet.

WHEN WE WERE THE "OTHER"

For my Italian American friends wearing MAGA hats. This is the voice
of your forefather, my forefather. He was a young man then.

We carried pots and pans on our backs like circus tents
Our hunger could be seen in the other's jawbones
We boarded boats that broke paths in a vast ocean
I was excited to watch the ocean foam
Then one day, land appeared
On deck we clapped and smiled
Shared what remained unspoken
And some of us made it to a sun-kissed bayou
We smelled salty marsh air in the morning
Caught jumping catfish with our bare hands
The girls ground Sassafras with mortar and pestle
The girls smelled like orange peel back home

One beauty lay lolling in the sun
It all happened at once—that first deep joy between us
She drew her mouth towards mine. I knew her pulse
Under a cypress we were brokenness made unbroken
Unbroken my girl said when she kissed my fingertips
Then we went back to looking the way we did
Back to our shanties in a row
We'd named "Little Palermo," as a way of belonging
My mother bending over a coal stove
My mother smelling of Spicebush and Blue Eyed Grass
She foraged and dried wild plants to make teas
That woman could heal any sickness, except hate
When we were front-page news in *The Daily States*:
"Like the Negro only filthier in habit"
"A villainous looking set" terrorizing the nation

We were fruit peddlers, street sweepers, loading dockhands
We were juice for the Confederate President's speeches
Fuel for angry citizens preparing for action
We were Southern Italian too dark to be honest
Accused of killing Hennessy, Chief of Police

We were hundreds loaded into mule-drawn carriages
My girl shouted *reggiti, reggiti*, hold on, hold on
I held on to one strong shoulder
He asked me: *ma unni iammu?* where we going?
We went down past Tulane We held on

Whittled down to nineteen, then eleven
We were Rocco, Pietro, Antonio, Emmanuele,
Tony, Loretto, Bastian, Joseph, James, Frank, Charles
—Tried in court and acquitted
Returned to Parish Prison on "other" charges
And the bloodthirsty stormed in
And the warden turned a blind eye
And they all jeered and harangued: "Who Killa Da Chief?"
One of us whimpered: "Not Guilty"
One of us proudly replied: "I was born in Louisiana"
One of us stammered and cried: "I liva hia sixa yias"

We were nine "Dagoes" clubbed and shot
Lay weltering in blood and brains
We were two hanged on the lamppost off Treme St.
We were one riddled with 42 bullets after the dangling
We were others whose names disappeared from the record
One fled to Vicksburg and one to Tallulah
One clung to life when a tree branch snapped
And if it's true that our true selves emerge closest to death
Then my father took-in the cottonwood's tiny red blooms
Caught a glimpse of the mighty Mississippi
Had his memory of his woman in the sun
While the crowd found a sturdier branch
And the determined hurled him up a final time
And a dozen bullets put an end to his writhing
As his grieving son ripped out his own eyes
March 14, 1891—New Orleans

TENDER SHOOT IN THE PARK

By the drinking fountain a girl
picks wild violets
then runs by the flame she lives by
— one flower for her dog's ear,
one for her mother's lap, one for
her own unruly hair.
I want to wrap my arms around
the thrill of her thoughts.
I 've fallen in love with her perfect beeline legs,
one bandaged knee, small yellow chest
dressed to brighten gray weather.
Nothing on earth could get me to lower my eyes
except to search my notebook
for the bookmark of pressed flowers
I want to give her. Say
child of spring, Tender Shoot, this
for you, & isn't the heart so buoyant
so blissfully open
when we don't keep our eyes
& arms & what we love all to ourselves?

But I'd written a few words
to preserve what had marked my vision.
I looked up, around   Tender Shoot
had vanished like a morning star.

II

*I drink. I burn. I gather dreams
and sometimes I tell a story.
Because Promethea asks
for a bowl of words before she goes to sleep.*
—HELENE CIXOUS

THE WORD SURVIVES THE BODY
for poet Maria Marchesi, 1925-2012

Her suffering voice still circles
& rises from the roof
of Santa Maria della Pietà,
the old Roman nuthouse where Maria
leaned on windowsills, looked out
between iron bars,
called Life a whore
for dressing in splendor & sass,
for sprawling on sidewalks & public parks
to enjoy the sun, the breeze, the chatter
of children playing ball, for hiding
between the dew & lily of the valley

When someone in the woman's ward
said Life was last seen climbing
a rocking horse
spinning round & round
nibbling hard on her lip
lamenting: I'm hungry
Maria said she'd never managed
to meet her Life
but could make sense of the senses

Lacerations inside the belly —
old shiftless loss
so long, covert
it taxes the heart
like fireworks of rotted time
za za boom zazaboom
& it stinks
like the carcass of an abandoned cat
except when Spring
engulfs me in desire that hardens
the breasts, exalts the vagina.
When frogs sing from the riverbed
I shall wander the streets, naked.

One frog will learn of me,
see how beautiful I am & full
of ardor. He knows
even the wind can make me come

Shrinks in white coats laugh & shake
their heads, take turns
sticking fingers up Maria's ass.
She assures them she's joking.
White keeps good company
with madness. She's always found
black in her milk & her bed.
She dares the white coats to look at her
as if she were a woman, could reveal
the mystery of love & creation,
dares them to notice she lives on paper,
is but a word, a clue of life:
Between me & the light
is the possibility of immortality.

VERONICA FRANCO'S RANT

When I was a young wife, sugarplum
& corset elegance of primrose,
fresh victim of man-made law, forced
grown

— that garden
of order sacrosanct & deadly

how decorum
turned me bitter rhubarb, then led to my fame
Poet & Prostitute of Venice—*I wish it were not
a sin to have liked it so*

Tell & retell how love once born
of generous sentiment turns
ownership in marriage, & there
it is

face of corruption—tarantula
bedding you in threatening position, crawling
its way up your gut

The man
who once enraptured, now bored me
out of my mind

What I once called
the act of love became forfeit possession
Full with one food I longed to taste another—
how old is the gut's right to discover?

I stopped chasing divinities of my lawful mate,
charged him with abuse of comfort, too familiar

Not long ago I seduced him with just the sound
of my rustling skirt
ungloved hand

Poor guy
he too had been cut off from renewed hunger,
followed the law, & I doubt
he remembered what wild desire was.

COWARDLY

The heart once a child grows old
Forgets to uphold internal law
Develops irritable bowel syndrome
Shies away from eating *friggitelli* peppers
Shining like red bullhorns
Why risk another spike of heartburn
Feed yourself bland soup
No more forbidden behavior allowed
No being beaten & blown about
Complete bed rest. Right you are
There's nothing as peaceful as being walled-in
Days & nights are more predictable
Rust grows around you like a halo
One morning you'll wake paltry & gray
& hovering in the air
The smell of an old woman's underwear

LE MONDINE

Angels of bitter rice

Le Mondine barefoot bent over knee deep

across Italy's rice belt

Le Mondine tormented

by malaria-thick mosquitoes

Le Mondine with no cover of any kind for sleeping

Le Mondine 14 hours immersed in water by day

found the resolve to dance by night Le Mondine's sweet pride

like a punch in the face to men standing tall with their clubs

Le Mondine sleepy indolence of the strong

heroines of the left activism thrived in the paddies

River Po Valley

resounded with call & response *Ciao bella ciao, bella ciao ciao ciao*

Le Modine hundreds of thousands stronger than canons

did not go back to weed & harvest

brought Fascism to its knees

but something is shamelessly not right

the country they bled for

remembers the song of resistance forgets Le Mondine

natural resource, workhorses mothers of labor laws & human rights

IN THE READING ROOM

Turn to Boccaccio's third day first story —
to the bars at the door of a convent.
Masetto the gardener gains entrance,
poses as deaf-mute & deficient in intellect.
Masetto perpetually sexually hard
assures the Abbess he can't reveal
pleasuring an entire convent of nuns.
Such longing in the young nuns
on the hour, every hour, one goes in
to, one comes out of
the hut in the enclosed garden of love.
Worn-out Masetto finally speaks: *In God's name
let me go—one cock for ten hens is way too much labor.*

Still laughing I close *The Decameron*
but want to be dressed in more natures
as in Pasolini's adaptation— his swirl of
villagers, clergy & hustlers vomiting, farting,
their fucking bodies populating
Naples' underclass speaking their jargon
even the young have gaping & broken teeth.

Uncontaminated life
                              come in
turn on the desk lamp—set to work
to that inward flying
                                        to that fugitive poem
that leaves me hungering.

LOVE POEM

Where else to carry love but on the lips

I silently speak your name this time of sunset

The sun sinks its last drop of honey into the sea

I put aside everything about the day

Try again in words never large enough or small enough

Thank you for showing me that wondrous garden

Crown of dandelion scattering in the breeze like flying stars

The bluebird carrying on its back the blue of heaven

Even as the sky turns black, urges every knifepoint star

To shudder: *Greetings to the lonely bride*

All these internal verbalizations while the vigilant woman

Slips off her shoes, plants her feet in the garden of raw self

*

If not for you I could never write such whimsy words

This talk is indeed from another world

Like Eros keeping Psyche unconscious

You see, I've caught the worst of it

My soul has become the charlatan selling dreams

Mellowing the rain falling like pitchforks

Tearing apart the flowers & the hive of bees

Anyone who knows me would be shocked

To find I can't tell the sun from a ball of honey

A singing finch from a swollen yellow melon

A flaming-red peony from an exotic bird

As final insult my soul summersaults, spits out:

Floundering is sweet in such a field

*

You are sixty times the food of life

I want to look into your eyes & hear your voice

My bridegroom, you remain invisible

I still have troubling days robbing me of strength

To keep the kitchen table tidy, wash my bed sheets

There are recurring visions of a fish caught in a net

A knife slicing the creature in half

There are lucid moments & I manage to remember

I am the whole self within the self in creative life

*

I buy an atlas & search the forests, a floating bottle in the river

Spread a meal of nuts & berries under the shadow of a pine

My hair is let down & flying

In the grove of wish-fulfilling trees

At last, I find you in a fierce embrace of wind arriving

As the lake swells & earth is shaken, as the sea wildly foams

Look at that! I'm waking unburdened in the light of that dream

With the habit of thanks still in me, & a hunger for breakfast

OF ROSE I SING

for folk singer Rosa Balistreri, 1927-1990

Rose, sing of Pirates in Palermo
My hair stands on end
So many ships arrived—over millennia
Pirates stole the splendor
Left us in the dark
All the gold of oranges stolen
Countryside naked in the fog
Sea empty of its color
Fish crazy with lament

Rose, sing of Rabbit, Quince & Cherry
Find me raw with lust
The rabbit has a mouth
The rabbit has a breath
The rabbit has a foot
The rabbit has a chest
The rabbit has a belly
The rabbit has a fur
A new lover has the makings
Dream of him tonight
Mouth on mouth
Breath on breath
Foot on foot
Chest on chest
Belly on belly
Fur on fur
Rose, ask how the cherry smells
How the quince?

Rose, sing your Peddler Father
Let me feed you, sister

Rose, sing *Puttana di to Mà*
Stab that whore in-law & her puny son
Sing your jail sentence & strum your guitar
Break out in lonely but never listless song

In Florentine Squares & street curbs
Milan's symphony hall

In savage voice, mourner's wail
Sing Sicily's mystery & misfortune
Her magnificence & courage
So full yet frayed so thin
Rose, you are all these things
Iconic tunes of gloom & rapture

After 20 years in exile
Rose you're home to rest your bones

Of Rose I sing across time & ocean
Of Rose I sing

LADY & DANNY BOY

Who was she to me? A stranger I met one autumn night on a park bench. Another would have ignored her hankering to strike a conversation, but the full moon rose over Madison Square Park & established grounds for discourse. I claimed that lady twisting her hair with her fingers. Her eyes said I am spacious & dare not contain what is inexhaustible, like music

Like the soul that comes rushing
from the same source as the body's power

Like a garden can't withhold itself from the sun
she met him again in a nameless restaurant

Their appetizer arrived. One first served the other
as if giving & receiving holy communion

As if spring lettuce & heirloom tomatoes
could erase the ancient curse of desire

She wore a dress of loose cotton.
She watched the old chase of his eyes

Maybe, she thought, it was time he came closer
in some forest, some makeshift cabin

behind stalks of corn, some way
of waking & sleeping, some way of

shivering & watching how well
spring rain brings on the grass

Our lady's trance was broken. She heard him say *Why not preserve it.* Had the man read her mind? Did the fickle night represent two aims, two sides? Was theirs a spiritual union? Moonlight flickered across the lady's face & she replied that even unappeasable sadness gives up to love. Then she braced one creaky knee, rose from the bench humming a tune I recognized: *O Danny boy, from glen to glen & down the mountainside.*

CATARINA SAGURANA

She lived in Nizza, once & seven times shuffled back & forth between France & Italy. The villagers called her *Maufaccia* (ugly face) but Catarina Sagurana paid no mind to gossipers with time on their hands and better off than a washerwoman & her fisherman husband.

Catarina budgeted her time strictly. She left her tent at dawn, carried heavy baskets of other people's laundry down to the Paillon River & beat dirty into clean with her big sturdy paddle.

Catarina acquired extraordinary muscles.

When armies of the Catholic Majesty King joined forces with the Muslim Sultan, the Magnificent, the deal to pillage another Mediterranean village was sealed. Just as a Turk was unrolling his flag to plant on the tallest castle tower, Catarina ran up the hill like a relay runner, wacked the invader with her wooden paddle & sent him spinning down to the water. She was quick to grab the flag.

The washerwoman turned her back to the stupefied soldiers below, hiked up her skirts & exposed her bare bottom. Determined, she squatted— did her thing— wiped, & flung the soiled flag in their direction. This so repulsed the men's sense of decency, they fled. A village was spared if only for a day.

For hundreds of years treaties were signed & nullified between dukes, popes, and self-crowned bullies. The people, bruised brawlers, were confused. Were they Savoyard (Italy was then The House of Savoy) or were they French? In 1860 Nizza became Nice, & the people began to munch on their baguettes.

It's the 25th of November 2017. On Vieux-Nice the pastry shops glisten with decadent buttery croissants. The sun shines on all sides and the sea sparkles azure. Wreaths are laid on the bas-relief monument of Catarina Sagurana, Catherine Segurene, as she's called in Provencal. A play unfolds, Commedia Dell'Arte style. Today we remember to laugh, remember the imposing power of a woman's ass.

IN A ONCE WHALING VILLAGE,
THE RECOGNITION

I enter a historic house with scalloped shingles.
Climb two flights of stairs to a railed rooftop.

In a former life I must have loved a sailor lost at sea.
Why else would I meet myself on this widow's walk?

The wild Maine sea is sighing its ecstasies.

ZAGARELLA, WHORE OF BITETTO

After Antonio Rutigliano's play: Metatron

400 years ago in the province of Bari
I walked Bitetto's streets in veils & pearls,
hair red as rose adorned with *zagara*

on my bed Persian covers
on my neck French jewels
my mouth open as desert flower
tongue dueling at once with two lovers
& my words sweet as ripe olive
for Francesco sinning with me

Chorus: *Zagarella with citrus flowers in your hair*
leave our village, let Francesco be

For wanting to possess all of me
I once refused Francesco, threaded braids afresh
& hit the street for new prey—his son.
Poor Francesco, terror seized his soul.
He plunged deep into my swollen womb

Chorus: *Zagarella with devil child*
burn in everlasting fire

After the Holy Inquisition burned my body
Rabbi Samuele from the Hebrew quarter testified
I often went to him speaking Arabic & Greek,
came face to face with my Creator,
entered end of correction, the 125 degrees
& further inquiries uncovered Francesco is
my father, & his son—my brother. I am
Enoch, Metatron, Christ & Antichrist.

The Altos Rise: *Eternal Mother full of glory, mysteries & immensities*
Glory in the father & glory in the son
For every man contains every woman as well

The Basses Bellow: Glory in the whore's spirit
Wants everyone inside

SMELLING THE FOX

Long ago & yesterday an orphaned fox
Entered a lonely hunter's neighborhood

Removed her skin & became woman-wife
Cooked meals, cleaned house, mothered children

Arranged flowers for the table, made money
In advertising on 7th Ave.—like you wouldn't believe

The hunter thought his wife beautiful & so crafty
He'd placed his happiness in her hands

Looked at her naked body like a body of water
For twenty years the pair merged as wave as sand

But outside of bed he complained about her smell
Could she peel off that underlying wild musk?
Tattoo his name & rank on each of her breasts
Where's my this & my that, the food's too peppered

Got so bad, his wife schemed the perfect crime
Her mid-life brain caught feral fire

She remembered foxes smell like violets
& she turned & turned depleted in her bed

Until knowing was ripe—a dream—a tree
Heavy with apples: *Eat, creature of appetite*

Her soul beneath the sheets leaped out like a bean
Jumping & howling *Fox Fox Fox*

A hailstorm marked the road for her to follow
Deep into the forest—juggling apples on her nose

In the forest there is no deodorant. Foxes are foxes
Grace you with their presence.

THE MAN ON ECHO LAKE

From the remotest past he sat waiting
under a spruce—one side of Echo Lake

I could easily cross & reach
the man among pine needles gold as the sun

He held out his hand & I knew
we were twin souls could frisk the skies

There was a boat to take me across—
a four-star General stood beside it

Now then, I said, I will climb on
slip out of my panties—fling them overboard

Float to him ceremoniously
reclined, like Modigliani's Nu Couche`

Take yourself for a walk said the General
—step foot on the boat of trials

You & that man will go blind. If you touch
one finger, an explosive will detonate

Saturn will swallow your children back in N.Y.
You're a human grenade. Be sensible, he said

Have you rinsed the mason jars back home?
Plum tomatoes are $10 a case, & ripe for canning.

I HAVE NOTHING TO SAY SAID THE POET

Let me tell you something
said the endangered poet
if I'm cursed to no longer have
the gift of alterability, if
deprived of being *imbambolita*
—dazed with a wicked doll's eyes,
if my dog nose
no longer scrapes the ground
for the rabbit's trail & that
of every game-bird,
if I stop inviting quiet footsteps
into my house of secrets, & if
I dare send my love-muse away
to make trouble for some other
proper wife & mother
so well behaved & always on time,
I have nothing to say.

BLOOD MOON

Have you raised your eyes?
Are we seeing the same sight at the same time?

A lunar eclipse this rare, not for another 18 years
All the sunrises & sunsets that ring the world

I've taken to sky gazing again
Avoiding the nightly news

There will always be crying to do
Someone ending in love, war, fight within

Someone getting back up in private struggle
Making neighbors of us all

I could feel absolved if I cling to life's limitations
What am I telling you? I loved you the best I could

I watched a bird fly home to the cavity of its apple tree
Heard the murmur of a flowing brook

I planted moss & lush roses on windowpanes
Time & again knocked out

I could not tell you from the bird, the brook, the roses
Have you raised your eyes, my mislaid love?

This blood moon will not be willed away
Such cosmic beauty agitates the heart

All the world's radiance once flowered & bound us
Once we were a mess of tangled honeysuckle

Forgetting the temporality of all things
All things on loan from the universe

Have we gone to weed?
Have we scorched each other to the root?

DONNAFUGATA

17th century castle named for a fugitive woman (Donnafugata, Sicily)

My name is Bianca of Navarra
but few remember my name.
I once saw a tranquil harbor, fishermen
on the rocks, dogs snoozing in the sun.
I walked in halls of Venetian mirrors
that equaled the Palace of Versailles
until a brutal Count seized my castle.
Spiders lay dying by my bed.
The night gave birth to flaming breaths
& brazen hooves of a bull.
I have seen the raging bull
lick his lips with an air of timelessness.
I have seen his nostrils flare,
his head & tail tear into my bones & marrow.
Faint as a bug on its back I was,
what more could I want but death.
A divine force flopped me over, & I
crawled the walls of an underground tunnel.
All grace all goodness was sister moon
lighting the way to the rolling countryside.
Ficus, carob, cluster of pine said it would soon
be spring, & I smelled that sweet night air
with a startling intensity I had never known
for whatever I loved that moment
seemed to celebrate my flight.
My name is Donnafugata—castle, village, endless
rows of grapevines—sparkling reds & whites.

HOW THIS DARK GIFT

Prisoners eating our rations at the dinner table
after a long marriage we faced our tiny horror

In a world of larger thorns we were but a speck,
swallowed hard in tight-lipped smiles—
kept talking

One low voice said: "It's over"
the other shouted: "Fix the bathroom faucet"

The flat roof leaked   We wrung wet rags in the sink

Cows everywhere had been lean for more than seven years

Would we slaughter them?

Show compassion for our failures while we still stood?

With loud sobs I threw my arms around him
as if his casket were about to close

He stroked my hair, kissed my mouth, gripped my hands —
what happened? What happened?

How to explain
states of change when I was barely breathing

Who cut down our tree, fed your heart to a fire
He yelled, I whispered—must be some god's idea of a joke

We were smoldering embers preparing to disperse
onto unknown air, & I knew so little how this dark gift

would give me wings. Navigate the world, alone?

The closer I got to that unknown place in my head
the less I asked for directions

that February night of lovers ended with no roses,
no pulse of untroubled sighs—a Valentine's Day massacre
but we had finally looked up & into each other's eyes.

SNAIL WORLD

green turned mud in the land of grazing sheep
cow bells swung as wind chimes
crawlers left trails of slime on leaves

once the rains were outward bound
the countryside renewed with children
& women in bare arms

hands combing dewy leaves for snails
that would be dinner
I bow to you snail coming to the surface

snail world of slime & nourishment
snail world of never eternal bliss nor constant pain
I bow to your cluster of peculiarities

I bow to your strong muscular foot
I bow to your primitive brain
snail world of hard shell & soft body

return me to instincts of survival
so I don't drown

TAKING LEAVE

Let down my hair to cover my face

I have no black veil & must descend

Open to pain I fear the greater pain of forgetting

That rape was not war   Don't ask me

Did I see the waste of his life   Did I accept my fate

It was not war but I could not stop dying

Now I wait for the luxury of contemplation

In the underworld of deceptive dreams & aborted hopes

Let down my hair long as a curtain

I can't squander my days of passage

Let no hand extend to interrupt this grieving scene

In other words

Leave me the hell alone with the devil

For not until

Trees reduce to pitiful twigs, & someone

Shuts off all the springs that feed the land, & rivers

Dry to muck & sediment, & of course

I shall never have proof

That facing the dark leads to light

BATTLEDRESS

Kinswomen uncover your scars
whether slight   still oozing   or deep pit

Brocade of bruised strawberries, blood covered rubies,
pale pink Chantilly lace

Call on the muses to seam them
into a battledress

Add a long train of fiery bird feathers

Hang your dress in the closet
as proof of pleasures & failures survived

Should your soul, one day, wake frozen but famished
means you've outlived a dawn
more hopeless than midnight with no moon

You've looked into your quiet mirror
& something that wants to live
begs

Open the closet   Slip on the pelt   Write!

III

I am not afraid to be memoir
—TOI DERICOTTE

ANISE SEED

The plant had been dried & beaten to make the seeds fall

She brought a jarful from the old country

There would be holiday cookies & anisette liqueur

There would be a back yard for growing fragrant herbs

After her husband died the jar sat unopened on a shelf

One day I asked my mother if those seeds hadn't dried out

One day looking as if she were in a hurry

She wrapped a few kernels into the dirt behind my house

Then rocked back & forward

    Heart-shaped leaves in spring

    Explosion of white flowers in July

    Condiment for soups & stews

    Tea to soothe my crying babies

    Oil to rub on my mother's knees after radiation

    Wash for red & swollen eyes

My mother's hand has vanished but is active

Just so, you come to wake me anise seed

As I do the most American thing there is

Eat lunch alone

Today it's pea, fava & stalks of anise soup

BENEATH THE CASTLE'S VAULT

Relieved from bowing in submission
two young girls removed their veils,
ran out of Sunday Mass
like ponies with free flowing hair.

They passed the black statue
of San Teresa in the churchyard,
white lilies at her feet
mercilessly wilting in midsummer sun.

Two girls throbbed with dream
all the way to the abandoned castle
for a game of statuettes —
hearts somewhere between
what they inherited & ran away from.

When anticipating life to come
we forgot to be mortally small.
My friend Anna with stolid attitude
forgot to stutter. In flowing speech
she commanded: Chiona, rise—

Snow Goddess in upturned look
glowed as I imagined a frozen river —
colorless, scentless, a sacrificial element.
I asked who would dispel the sorcery,
a prince on his white winged horse?

Bracing a Corinthian column
in her own good time Anna answered:
"The royal horses have left with all the nobles.
My savior is a mule."

Anna could dream on the mandate of reality,
unload her heaviness on a poor beast
the Vittorese called dumb-witted ass
that carried the world's weight.

Goddess & mule magically flew
across the turbulent Straight of Messina,
left all the damned peasants behind
for the mainland.

What did we know about
Hansel & Gretel, Sleeping Beauty
or Dr. Seuss?

We lived & breathed Greek myths
our barely literate mothers recited at bedtime
& we learned the anguish of the human world.

When we weren't Goddesses,
when we weren't hiding
from girls idling in doorways
lowering skirts past bony knees,
we watched women unleash
buckets of water on sidewalks,
settle the hot noon dust
in our Baroque village laid out on a plain
like an old man in ruin.

So many flying images before my eyes
once trapped in the net of memory
—mothers kneading bread, shelling almonds,
scrubbing bed sheets in wash-sinks,
some days their cracked knuckles bled.

Anna & I helped fold the wash
that had stiffened in the sun,
sprinkled sea salt on sliced tomatoes
put out to dry on the balcony,
preserved whatever fruit was in season —
licked hot spoons of sweet marmalade
just as the quince began to harden.

IN THE HOUSELESS LOT

Serpents need something to rub against when they shed skin,
sharpen their sights & smell with their tongues

I was mesmerized. Anna knew so much & stitched together words
      fluidly as a fine seamstress stitched hems

Unless Anna stammered & continually blinked
      then she went from brilliant girl to ordinary beast growing claws
      — wiped out what spiders had worked all night to spin

& I was fearful of the way destruction never looked so beautiful
      in the houseless lot where thorny plants grew
         I stared at spaces between Anna's teeth

I stared at her fingers tearing spiny heads off cardoons.
      I stared at two cats brushing their fur
         against the legs of an abandoned table

One went down, raised her tail, the male hissed & bit her neck
      from behind. My face gnarled in disgust—or was it
         oscillating between pleasure & offense

Anna shot back
    Take off that dumb mask; cats do what is natural for cats
      & you're a S S S S tupid little girl
         if you don't get closer to their smell

CASTAGNO DEI CENTO CAVALLI
The Hundred Horse Chestnut Tree, 2,000 years old, Carpeneto, Sicily

We came upon the famed tree
on Lingualossa Road
at the foothills of Etna.
My father's strong hand in mine
now blurred blue residue.

Papà, perchè l'albero si chiama così?

I received the legend
while becoming the legend:
Queen of Aragon caught in the fury
of thunderstorms saved her 100 knights
on 100 horses under the chestnut tree.

My young heart turned so old
under that massive roof of leaves.
Face up, face down, I was dressed
in golden dress & crown,
battled lightning & thunderbolts,
rescued rocks, bird bones, broken twigs,
carried them safely out & set them free.

LAST BIRTHDAY WITH MY FATHER

He tipped the brim of his fedora down low
to shadow his hollow cheeks

I thought he drank the autumn wind
I thought perhaps the world ends here

His nut-brown complexion turned chalk-white
like an aristocrat who'd never seen the sun

His lips on my forehead were cold but moved
if they emitted sounds that meant happy birthday

I didn't hear as I was pulling & twisting
the wool flannel of his leg

He stepped into the ambulance,
elegant & dignified as ever—as I see him now

Gray hounds-tooth blazer draped over his shoulders,
legs spread to endure their otherworldly flight

A crowd of strangers gathered by our front door,
the Myrtle Ave. L shook the room where I was left

empty hands dangling at my sides,
crippled legs dragging me outside

The ambulance sped until it faded
I cried out but the voice was stuck inside

The street a minefield—Dead leaves
danced on the ground. Dead leaves danced in the air

Would there ever be a better birthday suited
for despair, fraught with such terror

"This is" your first year in America.

PIECE WORK

The pocket-maker earned three cents apiece on Harman Street,
        three cents per coat pocket in the 1960s.

At night she sat with carpal tunnel in both hands
        yet did the math on our kitchen table.

So much for the rent, so much for her dead husband's
        blood transfusion to be paid on installment.

Had you opened the door & entered our dimly lit room
        you would have seen the shadow of my mother, 37.

Not her creamy skin, chameleon eyes, but what the gods
        had turned into Hecuba, a barking dog pulling her hair out.

We have No home, No language, No family, No way to live
        & after hours of exploding into her handkerchief

you would have seen her determined to create. Unfold a yard
        of coat lining she'd *borrowed* from the sweat shop,

make a pattern rise out of her head, move to pedaling
        the sewing machine, & there was a song from her youth.

Something about owning bits of daily life, under her breath
        was the sweetest song as if to distract destiny.

Her hands pinning the hem of an accordion-pleat dress,
        her daughter in tiptoes on a footstool

turning in baby steps, taking hold of a new self assurance
        & what went unsaid when the song ended:

Mother, I can't pinpoint when I became a dancer on that stool.
        Was it during or after you turned polyester into silk?

I shone like a ruby. You were beautiful as the moon.
        How long could hallucinations hold out?

ON THE ROAD TO CAMERINA

In the morning hours of a fertile spring that verged on summer the fields were a riot of red poppies, yellow sorrel, dusty-blue borage on the road to Camerina. It was easy to pick a bouquet of 50 different wildflowers. A Sunday ride on the Vespa with my father—speeding by remnants of walls made of irregular stones bound with mortar, a slight drizzle falling, warm wind in my hair. We stopped at a café for a glass of almond milk, took a stroll along the shore and found a bronze coin the sea had once concealed. I wouldn't know the origin of that coin, wouldn't know enough Sicilian history. I did what a child does—toss the coin back to the sea, make it skip like a rock and see how far it goes.

2,500 years of crossroads—warriors sailing with mighty armies acclaimed themselves Kings of Sicily only to be butchered by the next tyrant with a mightier army. Sicily and her people nicely dammed and left in ruins. Such a rich and bloody legacy, a kid could find the coin of her ancestor still damp and wrapped in seaweed—the people's sufferings, pity and pathos, as well as ageless rites, colors and celebrations. The coin I found, you understand, was before the excavations in the area of Punta Secca and Casuzze began in earnest, before the remains of a temple dedicated to Athena were revealed—now housed in The Archeological Museum of Camerina, or Camarina, or Kamarina or Kaukana. The locals still can't agree on what to call their village that changed names according to the language of the colonizer, never mind the Museum.

MOUNTAIN AIR AND HONEY FINGERS

Ragusa's hilly countryside was dotted with cows, farmhouses and trees laden with fruit. We were leaving the hills and what my father called mountain air. He claimed that mountain air "opened" the appetite and might lesson the sickly pallor localized on my face. I breathed more mountain air than the goats but was still anemic. Today I know that condition as Thalassemia Minor, an inherited blood disorder. The ancient disease has everything to do with geographic location, history of malaria, wars, invasions, mass migrations, Greeks, Carthaginians, Vandals, Goths, Pisans, Moors, Normans and Spaniards. I'll never need Ancestry.com, and the good news is my DNA has a survival advantage—flooded with so much malaria-laden-semen I'm immune to malaria.

Marisù, my father calls me through the waves of time, *Marisù*, we're late but almost home. When we get around the corner from the house, we'll walk. *D'accordo?* Don't tell your mother our little secret. I went along with his lie. We ran out of fuel and had to walk the Vespa home. Sorry, Lina. The *Benzinaio* was closed. I nodded, for this was certainly true. No gas stations, pharmacies, grocery stores were ever open during the sanctity of lunch hour followed by the necessary nap.

Lina, is lunch ready? We're starving after being out so long in that fresh mountain air, isn't that right, *Marisù?* How persuasive my cunning father could be with his subliminal messages. I would eat a fair portion of whatever was being served, but never an animal's liver. What other than liver could build iron rich blood? I saw the gravity, the deep lines furrowed on my parents' foreheads. After our meal his voice would go down to a whisper: Lina, did you prepare the oil and the syringe? The oil and the syringe was the torture I had to endure twice a week—B-12 injections and cod liver oil to drink for the anemia. My mother chased me around the house for what seemed like hours or until exhaustion overtook me and I surrendered to the long needle in her hand. My father tenderly held my face between his hands. In a soft voice he asked if I remembered the white caper flowers we'd seen crawling along a wall that morning. Before I could picture caper flowers she had rubbed alcohol on my butt cheek and the syringe had done its job. As for the oil: he pinched my nose to lessen the smell. I swallowed a glassful and didn't cry. I waited to suck on my mother's fingers dipped in honey. Her honey fingers replaced the taste of liquid sardines. I have almost forgotten the nauseating fish burps and the burning, throbbing pain in the ass. But a woman like that, and a man like that, how could I live without them.

THE PALAZZO ON VIA BIXIO

I left Anna in our abandoned castle one spring day, 1961. Her mouth wide open, her large dark eyes fixed on something out of this world. She was kneeling on a marble step of the grand staircase in her blue and white seersucker dress. Anna was spellbound, embodying Arethusa in a pool of papyrus. She had shunned Alpheus, River God, and he had split the earth, dug a tunnel under the sea from the Peloponnese to Sicily in search of the nymph he loved. With all the rush and power of a river he turned Arethusa into a fresh water spring to drink her eternally. (So one myth goes.)

The real spring of Arethusa is in Piazza Archimede, one of Siracusa's most celebrated sights in Ortigia, the ancient port city. At the center of a large art nouveau fountain stands the statue of Diana, Goddess of the Hunt, in all her calm, bearing witness to Arethusa's metamorphosis. Tritons prance about on seahorses.

Rarely did Anna and I suffer the curses of male gods or bow to their demands when we played inside our castle. The light went out that day when my friend said yes to being sacrificed and posed as Sicily's most beloved Goddess. Who could I have been when all appeared hypnotic? I burned to be Medusa—winged female with snakes for hair. I wanted to smell everything with my tongue. I liked Siona, Goddess of seduction in full womanly form, fruit and flower garland for hair. She held a dove in one palm, a ball of twine in the other. I liked her, beautiful enough to break your heart.

It could have been this or it could have been that, youth perceives itself and rejoices, says Italo Calvino. I say sometimes it doesn't. Chances are my stick-thin body wasn't playing at all on that day of reckoning. I was intently watching Anna in her pose and silently sobbing with sorrow. The previous evening I'd learned my family and I would be leaving for America in a few weeks. My incurable habit of allegory may be no more. No more than a soundless voice.

IN MY HOMETOWN

The street lamps kept dangling from disrepair, the balconies crumbling, the unemployed young men shuffling from café to aimless walks, yawning even in their thoughts—a scene worthy of Fellini's neorealist film, *I Vitelloni*. Fellini at his ironic best sets overgrown teenagers in a coastal town, a band of young bulls taunting road workers and pulling immature pranks on girls and women. My father said his kids needed a different future. Frasca Studio would soon close and one more family, my family of four, would become a statistic of the Sicilian diaspora. I had never heard the word "diaspora" until I came to America. In my hometown that history was not taught in school, far as I know. People just left. Like seeds transported by the wind one day they disappeared. Occasionally I'd hear my mother say that so and so, the American, was in town. That so and so could have a surname familiar to us, or one that had been Anglicized. The mysterious Mr. Nicholson might be searching for a distant relative—Nicosia.

We saw types on the streets of Vittoria during summer months. Mr. Nicholson in plaid shorts, white sweat socks and laced-up spectator shoes, walking with a small dictionary in hand—trying his best to ask for directions to somewhere his fourth cousin might be living. Anna & I made fun of that guy. What was up with those tube socks paired with elegant leather shoes? But his Ray-Bans were more than acceptable to two girls wanting to tint the world a splendid green. O how we wanted to rip those aviators off the foreigner's nose and take turns sporting them at the beach. Leap from one rock to the next, lean on every yew tree, look foxy sniffing the northern wind—*Tramontana*—cool on the skin. And we'd throw in some Paul Anka —*Put your head on my shoulder, Baaaby*, feeling euphoric though we didn't understand the words. It's hard to convey how that singer's dreamy voice on my transistor gave rise to lidless imagination. Opportunity for a pose, look a bit coy. Tilt your head. There. No. It was better before. Keep the sunglasses in mind. Can't you think of something more miraculous?

Here and there we'd see another American but demanded nothing from the Showoff, *Buffuni*—one hand pushing back his thick swirls of hair, the other spread on the steering wheel of a Peugeot convertible too big for cruising our narrow streets. The *Buffuni* wore his shirt unbuttoned.

His gold necklace was thick as a fishermen's rope. This clown made tons of money flipping pizza dough, my older brother said. One good bet he came back to look for a wife who cooks like his mother. She'll polish his shoes, his teeth, his nuts and his toenails just to get to Brooklyn or New Jersey. My eighteen-year-old brother, Aldo, who could not openly hold a girl's hand, carried around his little angry monsters and made Anna and I laugh until we almost suffocated.

If this isn't important, nothing is, Aldo said. In the beginning God created an American for us to see on Via Cavour. A nostalgic old man, teary eyed, in and out of cafés, tasting every flavor of gelato until the metal shudders shut. The bogus noble in suit jacket with the widest lapels you ever saw and polyester pants that never lose their crease, *U Babbu Amiricanu*, the Dumb American. All over town the air is thick with rumor that a speeding motorcycle flipped him in the air and he thumped on the ground like a 65- kilos sack of potatoes. Aldo could not get his mind off how mannish that violence was. Anna asked to hear more. My mother slapped herself hard on the forehead, called her son *Malacunutta*, a word I find impossible to translate. It doesn't mean not being polite—more like a fired-up entertainer setting hungry wolves to attack a poor captive bear.

I was nine years old, it was the place I happened to live in and be the victim of. What did I know about Mr. Nicholson longing to find his ancestral roots? What of those who had not quite died in the old country and not yet been born in the new, how they disassembled, reassembled, flying back and forth like the osprey's need to return to its birthplace. Each had a personal survival at stake but who could see any beauty in that? This doesn't quite answer the question: why are people obsessed with stereotyping? In my hometown we thought of all Italian Americans as "dumb" outsiders who dressed badly. They thought of us as their precious heritage.

THEATRICS

Did I hear church bells chime thirteen times—one o'clock—my mother expecting me for lunch? Did I go straight home with my head dangling like the street lamp when I left Anna at the abandoned castle for the last time, or did I turn for a final look at the *Sacro Cuore* and the swallows that endlessly circled the steeple as if those birds never thought of flying elsewhere? I often sang and danced my heart out, dressed as a pumpkin, in that church-auditorium. I have photographs of the pumpkin on stage. So many photographs of people in the act of clapping for a performer I recognize, head bowed, dressed as a daisy, a painted sun-dappled field in the background. Bees buzzed around clover and cows came along—not to swallow the bees, but to smile. I heard the neighbors say I'd become a Hollywood actor in my new land if that VISA came through. I know that my young eyes narrowed. Someone shot me in the head and legs. Why did hunters chase the blood trail and go straight for the heart? Why couldn't the American dream be realized in my little town?

Either way I would have bled to death. I was so tripped-up in lofty dreams of singing and dancing and everyone clapping for the rest of my life.

THE STREET OF LIGHTS

Twelve years had passed. The plane crossed the mainland, swerved and approached Catania. I caught the full sight of Etna rising like a dark sun. *A Muntagna* was quiet that day. A column of smoke kept dispersing in the sky. Alitalia's 747 landed and I got down on hands and knees, kissed the ground of Fontanarossa's airport from the sheer joy of stepping foot on native soil again. That summer, 1973, I was on my honeymoon. My husband gave me a strange look as I recall, and again I gave myself away as a sentimental fool on the two-hour drive from Catania to Vittoria. In a rented Fiat 500, our luggage tied to the roof, I pleaded with Peter to stop the car when I saw a tree heavy with fruit, a street vendor and his pull-cart on the side of the road, selling *Telline*, thumb-sized mollusks with the sweetest flavor. *When the sea was calm and I walked with my brother in shallow water we swept up Telline with scoop nets.*

What Hallelujahs greeted me when I arrived in Vittoria. Every evening I took walks on Via Cavour, dubbed *A Strata e Lumi*, The Street of Lights, blustering with a swarm of people exchanging pleasantries before arguing: Did you watch the San Remo festival on TV? They call that music? Remember Adriano Celentano's legs once all sparks and dazzle like Elvis, now it's long-face De Gregori for the sophisticated, nose-up-in-the-air Italians. They call him a poet. What's he mumbling about? Trains half empty and half full. *Merda.*

The conversation would turn to trains & how the *Littorina* was never on time when you most needed it. One woman whined about trains being cesspools and how a man had bumped against her with the excuse of the train's jerking motion. How she was mortified all the way to Palermo. Another revealed herself unguarded: "I was with you. I didn't see you draw back."

On The Street of Lights you moved while overhearing snippets of a stranger's life—marital complications, conflicts with children, and always the financial woes. Little had changed. Arm-in-arm I walked with four members of my extended family, battle chargers, taking up the width of the street. I still knew how to move out of the way if one or a chain of people needed to pass. *Buona Sera. Prego. Dopo Lei*, after you. The friendly fight erupting in a coffee bar could still be heard. One man shoving and shouting at the other for the privilege of picking up the tab, and even before that, a soft pastry wrapped for his friend to take home to the old mother.

Don't all people accustomed to their somber suffering need a Street of Lights? Strolling where only foot traffic was once allowed, reaching the end of the street that opened to the Piazza and the Villa beyond, taking a few moments to sit on a park bench, near the thick, low scrub, uncultivated vegetation that survived in endless dust, that had a silence you could hear, that followed you heading back in the opposite direction, towards home.

Where is home for the immigrant? I enter Italy as a tourist and will enter America as an alien with papers.

I often found my heart under a cobblestone on The Street of Lights. A young bride I was, teary eyed, dragging my husband in and out of cafés, *gelaterie*, tasting *nocciola, granita al limone con brioche*. Aunt Gina planting kisses on my face: *Amore mio*, how I loved to watch you snuggle in bed between your uncle and me when you were little. *Sangu mio*, you're so beautiful in that dress but if you're set on wearing it again tomorrow night let me at least iron it!

If the aunt I adored wanted to weave stiff bamboo into my linen dress and lose the fashionable wrinkles I'd paid good money for in America, who was I to argue? I was rejoicing in florid melodrama. My friend, Anna the ruthless, might have said: You've turned into that Dumb American we used to snub.

LETTER TO ANNA

I'm in New York up at sunrise at my desk with broken lion paws. I bought this old writing table at a yard sale. How to begin, dear Anna, after such a long silence between us, but to say the lion paws attracted me. They're broken yet manage to grip the ground. I can afford new furniture but allegory still likes messing with my mind. I have this nagging little problem. The dust of our abandoned castle has not settled and the image of your mouth wide open is a silent scream I can't seem to dismiss. I'm in a room of my own, a container for thoughts where the usual constraints of life don't apply. Here I consider the possibility of recomposing people. Here I become nameless, genderless, or inherit a multitude of names and identities. I am boundlessly insatiable like the naïve girl I was at the castle. I sometimes summon my long dead father and mother and get licked clean like a lamb in appalling human silence. Why not call you up from the dead, let the wind blow us back to the chaos that has always been spring. Hip to tender hip we'll walk by waves of oleanders, through courtyards with walls of roses, lemon trees thick with fragrance.

I enter this threshold if I strip away at the essence of my own being. You and I intuitively knew how to do this, didn't we, Anna, but had no words then to describe transcendence, just figured out what to do with free time and wriggled into play. This morning I'm in my body well past its prime and falling towards the underground. I'm reading Alexander Pope's epistolary poetry. Reading "Eloisa To Abelard" to you out loud. Are you listening, Anna?

> *Yet write, oh write me all, that I may join*
> *griefs to thy griefs, and echo sighs to thine*

I come with the part of myself that stands on the heartless staircase where we never said goodbye. Why did we never write? Mouth of sweet water, could the Goddess in you have predicted our futures. I've wondered, so many years I've wondered, if you ever returned to our castle—to be rescued by your own mind. If the times you pretended to be a powerful being shaped your brief life? I can't believe there's not another world where we will play and run high in the *Tramontana* wind.

I meant to write. I've told you over and over in my mind, I meant to write when the family settled. We never settled anywhere but into our losses. Before we could say in the name of the Father, of the Son, and of the Holy Ghost, my family disintegrated. At age eleven I became ninety-nine.

Step forward, tender flower, and I will tell you I have so few things left from the old world—nothing of yours. Only my memories remain to cap off our reunion. I would be an utter fool not to know that memories become distorted by time, yet somehow, and in the most imaginative ways, they help us fill a void inside. In the course of a life you encounter all kinds of situations which, seen through the eyes of a child seem more astonishing. What else? I have a few objects that are tangible. A book of photography with my father's handwriting on the first page: "Sviluppo: Metol 2, Solfito 2.5, Carbonato sodio 16, Potassio 1," measurements for the tank, and a footnote: dilute with 2 parts water during the warm season, only 1 part in winter months. What good are these instructions where the temperature is regulated and I'll never again develop prints in a darkroom, never again relish that acid smell. The meaning is in my father's handwriting that has travelled to the future, and implores—keep me close in the renewal and fresh start of your creative life.

Folded inside the book is a typewritten letter with an official seal from the Societa` Per Azioni, Milano, 29, 2, 1960, addressed to Famiglia Frasca, Via Vicenza 71, Vittoria, Ragusa. This is proof that I once had an address my mind hasn't made up. The letter informs that the submitted portrait "Girl with Almond Blossoms" has won the national contest. A monetary award will soon follow. Could be that substantial award money my father received for his artwork made our sea journey to America possible. I know that my mother's sewing machine stored in a trunk when we crossed an ocean saw us through the years that followed. The old Necchi is in my bedroom, the slide plate up, red thread still on the wind bobbin.

A dazzling moon is rising, Anna, full like a glowing disk, pale rose, copper rimmed, above dark water. Yes, it's night and I'm still at my desk. I watch the moon climb higher in the sky from an enclosed porch window that looks out at Peconic Bay. I'm in a clapboard cottage in Oysterponds, a hamlet on the East End of Long Island. Blue Point oysters thrive in these waters. Fishermen cultivate them rack-and-bag style in elbows of tidal creeks that bend off the bay. Farmers grow everything from asparagus that matures in April, to kale still hardy in November. I eat whatever is in season, like we did in the old world. The farms could never yield such bountiful harvests without hard working Mexicans who tend the fields. They live on the North Fork year round and work according to the calendar. The population here swells in summer months with city dwellers from different backgrounds. They own second homes in this area also rich with vineyards and an enormous lavender farm. When the month of June rolls around it can feel like Provence. But it's America where identity is ever changing. This place is so dear to me, some days I feel as though I had been born here. On good days I like to think of the larger America as a salad bowl that holds many ingredients. Each ingredient retaining its own flavor and mixing with others, then there's oil and vinegar, salt, pepper, so distinct one from the other, enriching the salad. Not everyone sees it my way and would like us all to taste the same or else kick us out of the bowl.

Every morning without thinking I walk the beach with my cup of coffee, pick up a veined rock with its unique fingerprints, admire a shell's curious mixture of iridescent blue and mother of pearl. Here is a whole world of blue at its unseen edges and great depths—sea and sky, making life expand into endless distances. Blue the color of emotion and longing. And so I set an intention like I set a new shell and a new rock on my writing table. Sit down to write, see where it takes me.

Now it's the season of silence. Beach chairs and kayaks have been stored away. The children have abandoned their sand castles and returned to school. The Greenport ferry heads towards Shelter Island and parts the water in silence. How good it is not to hear the engine's grind. I can barely see the outline of the boat. Strings of lights tell me it's a moving vessel. The silent journeys I watch in solitude leave me free to regard the ordinary and the imaginary—imperfect everyday life and the experience of different planes of being. To my right is Orient village, a long strip of land sticking out of the bay like a thin white tongue. A few house lights flicker in the distance. I imagine a woman switching-on her porch light, a child falling asleep in her mother's or her father's arms, a dog curled on a cotton-braided rug by the fireplace. Life looks idyllic in the shift-of-a-cloud. The illusion crumbles when my thoughts are drawn elsewhere. I'm waiting for you, Anna, to interrupt this monologue running on like a river. Maybe you are this cone of moonlight moving along the bay. I want your signal abolishing the complexity of personhood. And then ask me, Anna, why I never visited your grave on my many trips to Italy.

First, there's a mythological horse I want to talk about. Pegasus, the flying stallion that keeps himself busy saving others, carries around wounded soldiers. That horse we both knew in childhood tales also helped to shift the dead weight of a girl, coaxed her into climbing on its back. I swung myself onto the horse. Waited to re-learn how to live in this world. The view from up high began to expand a little. The horse would say things like: hold your head high, stop looking at the ground. Anna, it was the instinct to survive and a refusal to be pitied, but the horse and I were crawling through snowy wastes. Had I found some meaning in my mother's suffering? I had seen a dying chicken with the same look in her eyes. My mother's dresses had become loose, her back bent. She didn't care. I was the only one who saw and I was such a tiny stray dog trying to make up for my brother's absence. Aldo absorbed in his own desolation after our father's death, escaped to another city. Even his colorful and amazing monsters abandoned him. How can I blame Aldo, I had also fallen prey to that cheap temptation of knowing nothing and believing in nothing. In my late twenties I heard my young children breathing next to me and I feared what their lives might be if the horse and I failed to push forward.

Imagination had always been a friend of mine and I knew something about cloth and how to set a mood, impart an image. The profession led to travels throughout Europe. Florence became a second home and I know this sounds nuts, Anna, but I spent the sum of years in another castle, Palazzo Pitti, and Fortezza da Basso. In that Renaissance Palace south side of the Arno, and the fort inserted in fourteenth century walls, I pointed out artisanal properties of children's clothes to high-end American retailers. And there was the catwalk full of eight-year-old models. Kids trussed up in wares the likes of Armani Jr., Moschino, and Gucci. The loudspeakers blasted *La Bamba. Arriba arriba, yo no soy marinero, soy capitan, soy capitan,* what applause! Anna, what applause when the kids came out twirling in circle dresses, mint green, white crinolines, *La Bamba* written in Swarovski crystals hand-sewn across the bodice. Why not little girls as commanders of the seas? So proud were their wealthy parents at the Academy Awards. In Vogue and People's magazines they held their children's hands, harnessed the law of fashion trends. I drove the market.

I was flying so high, Anna, you might have asked if the horse had ingested magic mushrooms, I don't know, but I'm sure you would have called the Pitti Palace the castle of all castles. I am unapologetic of that life. Call it an immigrant's ambition. Did the actor in me surface when I spoke of my little garments? I handled fabrics that were so intricately woven, exquisitely tailored, I did think of them as small works of art. And the money was good. Money can buy you a room of your own, give your mother and your daughters a room to call their own. That's a whole lot of freedom for women.

Now I have Poetry. Poesia—a feminine word. Most times she's less rational brain and more irrational heart. Today she is paradox. For instance, your silent scream, Anna, scary and beautiful. I can't make sense of it yet the heart insists. What do you want from me, Anna?

I've been sitting here like a lone Christ in the desert and the devil shows me Florence. Beautiful Florence. But I'm not fond of a certain Square—Piazza della Signoria—though it expanded my consciousness when I worked for wages. On my way to the Uffizzi I was confronted with Cellini's masterpiece 600 years old and still on message in a world of male power. Perseus the hero and slayer, his exquisitely sculpted body holds a sword in one hand and the severed head of a dangerous female in the other. A stream of bronze blood exits the neck of Medusa. What do you want from me Anna? Yes, no one but you would know how much I loved making believe I was that dark mother that earned respect with her killer gaze. Isn't history told in its houses? The personal linked to the historical. The western world, but not exclusively, has always been at war with its women. Standing in front of Medusa dismembered, desexualized, spineless, I felt so feeble and all seemed to sink into insignificance—the scarlet flame of a woman burned out, her vacant stare and spilled guts. Such wretched statues as Cellini's Perseus drive nails into women's coffins. They bury us alive. They also force us into paying attention, contribute to knowledge; and knowledge is certainly progress.

Like an interior lake I want to be stimulated by the silence around me, see the sky change outline. The landscape in Oysterponds is a carpet of undisturbed snow. I've been anxiously waiting for the snowdrops, the flowers poets call milk and tears. They come up in February by the foot of an oak between the garage and the pebbled road at the edge of my property. I left this letter for a little while, went out to see a flower in the moon's luminous light. That snowdrop appeared so fragile—her slender stem, convex back and white head bent. An unknowing eye would be fooled by her humble appearance. Snowdrops emerge through snow and ice even before the crocus, wave furiously when a whip of wind tosses them about yet hold their ground and won't be pulled by the roots. Overjoyed at seeing them I wanted to take their beauty back to my desk. I could have snapped their stems between my fingers. Walking back to the house I pondered what language they speak, what sticky substance they bleed.

When the weather warms there's no shortage of wildlife speaking a language of their own—geese gawking, swans uttering hissing sounds from their windpipes, herons screeching when feeding their young. Tonight I run an eye on two quiet seagulls standing on one leg, top of the peer facing the lighthouse. Their heads are tucked under and all I see is their gray wings. What did the world do to cause the dissolution of these birds? It's not just the cold. They look like widows waiting for their husbands to return. I wish they would fly, show their spectacularly white underbellies and dive-bomb headlong into the open sea.

I don't understand birds any more than I understand flowers or the core of the sun.

I've taken off my galoshes, un-balled a pair of warm socks for my cold feet. The clock marks the eleventh hour. What language does the human heart speak? Is it loudest when suffering? Oftentimes mine is like a violin that has broken one of its strings. How to play melody on three strings? The great challenge is to make music out of what remains. And when I have only a rudimentary sense of existence I must think of what the Goddess Siona holds in her hands—dove and ball of twine. Anna, of wisdom I know nothing.

I did come back to see you but you were gone. A pop star sang a song on the car radio. *La Lontananza è come il vento, spegne i fuochi piccoli e accende quelli grande.* I heard that song that speaks of distance, how the wind puts out small fires and ignites large ones. I had more questions than answers and all I know of that car ride in 1973 is the song and my uncle talking about a brain tumor, your family moving North in the late sixties to give you better medical care but soon returning home to bury their only daughter.

Anna, have you been waiting for me to say that I knocked on the door of our castle? The oleander in front had been cut to a stump. I never felt heavier and more confused, impatient to go in and also wanted to pull back. I knocked on the door with the lion-head knocker—the same open-mouthed lion we knew, but the brass shone. The door was a rich mahogany. An elderly gentleman opened the door and I timidly said excuse me for disturbing, would you mind if I took a quick peek inside? My childhood friend and I used to play in this palazzo. We called it a castle.

The kind man invited me in and I stepped ever so softly as if I were entering consecrated ground. I soon learned that he was an architect and I smiled at the thought that someone could love that façade of cracked stone enough to restore it. Signor Ignazio insisted I remain for coffee when I introduced myself with my maiden name. You're the split image of your father, he said. He took my hands in his and let me know he had attended a Mass given in my father's memory a month after the voice spread that Signor Frasca had died thousands of miles away from home. There were no empty seats in Vittoria's Cathedral and not many dry eyes. The priest asked his parishioners to remember the Frasca family and filled the church with smoky incense. The church was all lit up with candles. Signor Ignazio spoke those words as if he understood my thoughts. God how I wanted to kiss that man's hand, how my mind shifted back to a funeral home on Greene Avenue, to a wake where only three people sat dressed in black. One heart-shaped wreath of red roses stood on wire legs and a funeral director doing his job paid his respects.

I was led into a small kitchen and watched Signor Ignazio open a drawer, select a few photos of his children in communion clothes. See? This is Elena. Here is Carlo. The photos confirmed what I already knew. I recognized the hand-painted photographic backdrop with faux finish, the sponged light and dark tones my father had painted in our studio. Then I discovered Signor Ignazio's great wound when he pointed to a black and white portrait of his deceased wife on the kitchen counter. His languorous eyes said he still ate meals with his beloved and his hand trembled while pouring more coffee into my cup. I helped myself to another bite-sized almond biscuit and inquired about his wife. In the portrait she appeared so youthful. Had she died young? He shook his head no. I didn't press for an explanation. It was plausible he wanted to remember her as she was in that photo, immortalized in health and a delicate smile.

Anna, I have never visited your grave on my many trips to Vittoria. It was not so much lack of courage at seeing your image on an oval ceramic, as the cemetery itself. A place we never went to. A world darkened by others. It would be like acknowledging our last tie. One summer I got as far as the entrance gate but decided to sit under a tree, my knuckles turning white. Who can ever really bring back what no longer lives but I can see a tree put out new leaves. When I gaze at a budding tree it often brings me back to a mental country from which I was once expelled. And I go back to the ocean my young self almost drowned in, figuratively speaking. It has taken me some years to fish that girl out. She emerged fragmented and exposed to the frost of her most unhappy of ages. On closer inspection I'd say she now wrestles to put out a few new leaves, feels more connected to a larger entity, and death loses some of its sting. Like your silent scream, Anna, is losing its sting as I keep writing, investigating, trying to make meaning.

Had you ever counted the number of windows we looked out of? I counted 24. All the shattered glass was gone, the windows brand new, the peeling walls restructured with white plaster and sandstone. The architect gave me a grand tour of his home and I took my time, stood silent and still as stone in spots where we once stood as shape-shifting figurines, quiet and undisturbed, considering how to hoist ourselves up. Our hands positioned just so in the air as if we were part of the very sky. I stood on the second floor landing, on a step of the white marble staircase, under the frescoed ceiling that now had uninterrupted pastoral scenes. Passing my hand on the balustrade I swear I had an overwhelming urge to slide down, reach for your hand as I explored the polish of fresh things. Is it possible to be so awed and terrified at once? Back then I never wrote a word of how possible it is to be in two places, two time zones, how to make the invisible visible, call someone who is absent into presence. I am telling you this, Anna, because you and that castle are responsible for my writing life. I have not known this until today.

Now I'm afraid I can't bear losing the creeping thorn-bushes that once encroached the old splintered door and the chipped tiled floor littered with bird droppings, and you lifting breadcrumbs from your dress pocket to feed a skinny stray cat, strike up an acquaintance with its gray fur that had collected all the dust of the streets, roofs and terraces. Your aimless walk back and forth, waiting for a Goddess to appear and take over at any time, turn that scrawny cat into the Queen of Sheba with emerald eyes.

Are you surrendering to a half smile, Anna? Everything is being stored in a "cloud." Can you believe that a computer screen sucks up and records all my mental activities? This technology makes my head spin like a cement mixer. The things I recall, feel, type and then erase—past and present—stored in a cloud. All the times I wrote I love you Anna, then deleted the lines, thinking how straight-out soppy, O yes, the flutter of kisses and goodbye embrace I failed to give you the last day I saw you at the castle. I'm sorry, Anna, I never told you how terribly I would miss you. I'm weeping because the bond of friendship is of supreme importance.

To have all this affection for another stored in a cloud? Why I ask myself, so I can be vigilant, protect the rational? Love rarely touches the reasoning part of the brain. I will not grow chilly. I will not chastise "sentimentality." Let others call the word smelly, almost indecent. I don't want my heart stored in a cloud.

Anna, our castle is the size of a four bedroom American house in the suburbs, just to put things into perspective and not spoil anyone's appetite for reality. An enormous joy laced with sorrow was that first visit (it wasn't the last). What an unshakable cry of the senses by the entryway when I kissed Signor Ignazio hard on the lips like he was my lost grandfather. I buried my nose in his shirt collar before leaving. The last thing I saw were two flowerpots I hadn't noticed when entering. They were made of concrete, verdigris, resembled urns with arms, tall—as tall as you and I were in 1961. I remember an ordinary delusion I had: *here, we are, preserved*—one to the left of the door, one to the right, a transition into another kind of existence inside a restored Palazzo on Via Bixio. Palladian windows let in the sun for the rosemary potted with upright geraniums. Varieties of jewel flowers with smaller heads spilled and trailed out of the urns. The architect knew his plants, and that long ago day was good for learning that rosemary is the herb of love, remembrance and myth. I drew close to one flowerpot and smelled the rosemary. I held one downcast flower tight between my palms.

Riposa in pace, mia cara Anna.

THE GREAT NORTHEAST BLACKOUT, 1965

The deep crease & contour of her eyelids,
the large oval mark
color of milk & coffee bordering her mouth
carried mysterious qualities.
Tommasa was the first friend I made in America.
We would know an abysmal night
—The Great Northeast Blackout, November of '65.
Traffic lights and streetlights extinguished,
police sirens rose & fell in ghastly wails.
We had learned enough English
to ask a neighbor about the lights.
Where are your mothers? Snapped the neighbor.
T. & I locked hands.
Sewing at the coat factory, one of us replied.
This further twisted our neighbor's nerves
& she explained about the lights gone out:
don't you know
your Guinea uncles cut the electric wires.
They're dumping bodies in the Gowanus Canal.
I took a step back
T 's jaw hung in awe-of-combat.
Her hairy facial spot stretched larger,
the fury of it strangely beautiful
like a tiger ready to strike.

      *

Then it was over.
Even fear & rage were rendered obsolete.
We watched a door slam shut,
climbed a darkened stairwell
in absolute silence
lost our breaths, looked for keys,
locked ourselves inside T's apartment,
lit two candles
as if
we were among the dying things.

THEME OF TOMMASA

Once was the grace of an immigrant girl.
In this song her name stands in for images
—her arms swinging,
her whole body swinging
a heavy mop on Saturday mornings
to spare the old Super with arthritic joints
from linoleum hallways of mosaic dirt
on Wyckoff & Myrtle.
The girl was born hungry to diminish despair
& the girl was born of poor musicians making do.
With eyes half-closed she blew across tops of empty bottles
to play flute,
wrapped tissue paper around her mother's comb of bone
for clarinet.
Let the long soft melodies
Let the sound of woodwinds also tell of her.

IN A COTTAGE BY THE SEA

I woke like a broadleaved summer tree.
My feet are set solid on a wide-plank kitchen floor.
My apron is splattered with eggplant & tomato seeds,
hands smell of mint, garlic & olive oil.
I stare out the window at a steely-blue bay
flecked gold by late afternoon sunlight.
My brother casts his fishing line, & I anticipate
a snapper's silverside beat against the bucket,
can almost hear the next wave lap against the jetty.
My husband is snoozing in a lounge chair,
my grown daughters splashing in the bay like children,
my gratitude for Earth's bounty & beauty
knows no bounds today.
When night comes on I'll cup my hands
around a flower that lights up in darkness.
This writing is critical
in the sixty-sixth year of my lucky life.

WATERMELON

I hold in my hands a slice of watermelon.

I hold within me entire summers,

orchards, seas & continents,

red juicy jubilance running down my chin.

Under the shade of a fig tree

I carry not the shade but the sun.

I carry the old street vendor by the roadside

Watermelon Watermelon,

pulp for eating, rind to polish your shoes.

Let me translate how some days

we live with a dual purpose

& in two worlds at once.

Some days loss is nowhere in sight.

YOU AGAIN

How the thought of you fills me with fragrance of baked apples &
cinnamon

How our fireplace on Peale Road crackles birch wood & tangerine peel

How I bend to open the oven door & check on the apples one winter's
day long ago

How you stand close behind me with spread hands bracing my hips

How I will not turn but linger eternally in that pose

OLD LOVERS ON THE HAMMOCK

Can you see us swaying on the hammock?

Hands raising two flutes—half filled

Our bare feet about to entwine

Think of the couple reclining in cushions

Our almond eyes shaped like those Etruscans

We once saw in Rome's Villa Giulia

That coffin covering terrified me so

I didn't like the lovers' terracotta braids

2,000 stale years braided together

No healthy marriage can last that long

I'm trying to build a moist, *living* portrait of us

Among fireflies perfectly satisfied pulsing their light

Moonflowers on the trellis without a care in the world

Your silver hair cropped & thin

Your arm confident around my waist thickened with age

I was once svelte & twice full of milk

& you with no baby bottles to fill

Waited to cradle our children in your arms

How the years accumulate

Through all the rhythms we've known

Our lovemaking so much softer now

The wind brings a faint scent of thyme from the herb bed

Smell of sea drifts up & the waves whisper *shush*

But dear Love

You can't help but sing to me in a gravelly voice

O What a Wonderful World

UNREACHABLE OTHER

Alone I stirred canned beans by the fire,
sipped tea to soothe a wringing stomach ache.
I loosened my hair from an imaginary ribbon.
Shall we go? he said, inside my wall tent.
We can still see the fire burning, the disordered stars,
or take walks to nowhere in particular
—so many moonlit nights. We can talk all night.
In the morning we'll rig up a tarpaulin for gathering rainwater.

What is your purpose? Unreachable other.
Are you the parts of me missing, the parts unknown?
Perhaps the feeling of never feeling settled?
Have I known you forever, would I know you if
all could be rewritten with new meaning.

Who is this "I" able to create scenes that delude?
Yet I hear the small animals of the woods
coo, screech & chatter, they trust
nature's open spirit. Sanctuary.

Dream traveler, we too are creatures of the wind.
Relax & float downstream
in the long intervals & intimacy of the water.
Drink the moonlight & let it
flood your eyes with the color of diamonds.
Like a prayer heard & answered
when your winged heart is at its loneliest
& knows the pain of too much tenderness
we'll be closer than we've ever been.

FLOWER ON THE BRICK WALK

The screen door banged behind me
The air was gray & dead
No sound of bird or wind
Just my shallow breathing
Maladies of the soul—shackles

Suddenly
           I couldn't breathe

A lone pansy raised her eyes
From razor-thin earth between two bricks
I mean
She was laughing so hard she was purple

The penciled mustard mouth
The smell of her
           Seemed to say:
               Come closer
               Listen to me

As soon as it starts raining

You must go

Where a pinecone breaks open & sprouts new life

Where crabs crack limpets' teeth clinging to the rocks

Gulls will butcher those same spider crabs

Nothing you can do about that cycle of slaughter, or the rain

The world is full of terrible & beautiful mutations

Like a pearl is by-product of disease

You're not done with your transformations

ACKNOWLEDGMENTS

Many thanks to the editors of the following journals and anthologies in which these poems first appeared or are forthcoming.

Yale Poetry Series Anthology : "Gazzosa" "The Golden Basin"

Making Mirrors: Writing/Righting by Refugees : "Under the Sky of Lampedusa, 2016"

From Everywhere a Little—A Migration Anthology : "Ode to Wild Fennel"

The Stillwater Review : "Fantasia" "Flower on the Brick Walk"

Voices in Italian Americana : "Anise Seed" "Of Rose I Sing"

Italian Americana, Cultural and Historical Review : "The Sewing School"

The Red Wheelbarrow : "Battledress" "You Again"

Luna Luna Magazine : "Veronica Franco's Rant" "In the Reading Room" "The Man on Echo Lake"

Kexaptun : "Between the Lions"

Ovunque Siamo : "When we were the Other" "The Great Northeast Blackout, 1965" "Poem of Exile" "Theme of Tommasa" "Watermelon" "On the Road to Camerina" "Mountain Air and Honey Fingers"

"Me Too" by Italian American Women: An Anthology of Poetry & Prose on Surviving Harassment & Sexual Abuse : "Smelling the Fox" "Taking Leave"

I am deeply grateful to Judith Vollmer, distinguished poet, dear friend, esteemed mentor, critic, and challenger. Magnanimous *Pazzarella*, from you I never stop learning and being inspired.

ABOUT THE AUTHOR

MARISA FRASCA is the author of *Via Incanto: poems from the darkroom*, and *Wild Fennel: poems and other stories*. Frasca holds a BA in creative writing from The New School and an MFA in poetry from Drew University. Her poems and translations have been featured in numerous literary journals and anthologies. She serves on the Advisory Board of *Arba Sicula*, a non-profit organization that preserves and disseminates the Sicilian language, literature, and folklore.

VIA FOLIOS

A refereed book series dedicated to the culture of Italians and Italian Americans.

RITA ESPOSITO WATSON. *Italian Kisses*. Vol. 136. Memoir. $14

SARA FRUNER. *Bitter Bites from Sugar Hills*. Vol. 135. Poetry. $12

KATHY CURTO. *Not for Nothing*. Vol. 134. Memoir. $16

JENNIFER MARTELLI. *My Tarantella*. Vol. 133. Poetry. $10

MARIA TERRONE. *At Home in the New World*. Vol. 132. Essays. $16

GIL FAGIANI. *Missing Madonnas*. Vol. 131. Poetry. $14

LEWIS TURCO. *The Sonnetarium*. Vol. 130. Poetry. $12

JOE AMATO. *Samuel Taylor's Hollywood Adventure*. Vol. 129. Novel. $20

BEA TUSIANI. *Con Amore*. Vol. 128. Memoir. $16

MARIA GIURA. *What My Father Taught Me*. Vol. 127. Poetry. $12

STANISLAO PUGLIESE. *A Century of Sinatra*. Vol. 126. Popular Culture. $12

TONY ARDIZZONE. *The Arab's Ox*. Vol. 125. Novel. $18

PHYLLIS CAPELLO. *Packs Small Plays Big*. Vol. 124. Literature.

FRED GARDAPHÉ. *Read 'em and Reap*. Vol. 123. Criticism. $22

JOSEPH A. AMATO. *Diagnostics*. Vol 122. Literature. $12.

DENNIS BARONE. *Second Thoughts*. Vol 121. Poetry. $10

OLIVIA K. CERRONE. *The Hunger Saint*. Vol 120. Novella. $12

GARIBLADI M. LAPOLLA. *Miss Rollins in Love*. Vol 119. Novel. $24

JOSEPH TUSIANI. *A Clarion Call*. Vol 118. Poetry. $16

JOSEPH A. AMATO. *My Three Sicilies*. Vol 117. Poetry & Prose. $17

MARGHERITA COSTA. *Voice of a Virtuosa and Coutesan*. Vol 116. Poetry. $24

NICOLE SANTALUCIA. *Because I Did Not Die*. Vol 115. Poetry. $12

MARK CIABATTARI. *Preludes to History*. Vol 114. Poetry. $12

HELEN BAROLINI. *Visits*. Vol 113. Novel. $22

ERNESTO LIVORNI. *The Fathers' America*. Vol 112. Poetry. $14

MARIO B. MIGNONE. *The Story of My People*. Vol 111. Non-fiction. $17

GEORGE GUIDA. *The Sleeping Gulf*. Vol 110. Poetry. $14

JOEY NICOLETTI. *Reverse Graffiti*. Vol 109. Poetry. $14

GIOSE RIMANELLI. *Il mestiere del furbo*. Vol 108. Criticism. $20

LEWIS TURCO. *The Hero Enkidu*. Vol 107. Poetry. $14

AL TACCONELLI. *Perhaps Fly*. Vol 106. Poetry. $14

RACHEL GUIDO DEVRIES. *A Woman Unknown in Her Bones*. Vol 105. Poetry. $11

BERNARD BRUNO. *A Tear and a Tear in My Heart*. Vol 104. Non-fiction. $20

FELIX STEFANILE. *Songs of the Sparrow*. Vol 103. Poetry. $30

FRANK POLIZZI. *A New Life with Bianca*. Vol 102. Poetry. $10

GIL FAGIANI. *Stone Walls*. Vol 101. Poetry. $14

LOUISE DESALVO. *Casting Off*. Vol 100. Fiction. $22

MARY JO BONA. *I Stop Waiting for You*. Vol 99. Poetry. $12

RACHEL GUIDO DEVRIES. *Stati zitt, Josie*. Vol 98. Children's Literature. $8

GRACE CAVALIERI. *The Mandate of Heaven*. Vol 97. Poetry. $14

MARISA FRASCA. *Via incanto*. Vol 96. Poetry. $12

DOUGLAS GLADSTONE. *Carving a Niche for Himself*. Vol 95. History. $12

MARIA TERRONE. *Eye to Eye*. Vol 94. Poetry. S14

CONSTANCE SANCETTA. *Here in Cerchio*. Vol 93. Local History. $15

MARIA MAZZIOTTI GILLAN. *Ancestors' Song*. Vol 92. Poetry. $14

MICHAEL PARENTI. *Waiting for Yesterday: Pages from a Street Kid's Life*. Vol 90. Memoir. $15

ANNIE LANZILLOTTO. *Schistsong*. Vol 89. Poetry. $15

EMANUEL DI PASQUALE. *Love Lines*. Vol 88. Poetry. $10

CAROSONE & LOGIUDICE. *Our Naked Lives*. Vol 87. Essays. $15

JAMES PERICONI. *Strangers in a Strange Land: A Survey of Italian-Language American Books*.Vol 86. Book History. $24

DANIELA GIOSEFFI. *Escaping La Vita Della Cucina*. Vol 85. Essays. $22

MARIA FAMÀ. *Mystics in the Family*. Vol 84. Poetry. $10

ROSSANA DEL ZIO. *From Bread and Tomatoes to Zuppa di Pesce "Ciambotto"*.Vol. 83. $15

LORENZO DELBOCA. *Polentoni*. Vol 82. Italian Studies. $15

SAMUEL GHELLI. *A Reference Grammar*. Vol 81. Italian Language. $36

ROSS TALARICO. *Sled Run*. Vol 80. Fiction. $15

FRED MISURELLA. *Only Sons*. Vol 79. Fiction. $14

FRANK LENTRICCHIA. *The Portable Lentricchia*. Vol 78. Fiction. $16

RICHARD VETERE. *The Other Colors in a Snow Storm*. Vol 77. Poetry. $10

GARIBALDI LAPOLLA. *Fire in the Flesh*. Vol 76 Fiction & Criticism. $25

GEORGE GUIDA. *The Pope Stories*. Vol 75 Prose. $15

ROBERT VISCUSI. *Ellis Island*. Vol 74. Poetry. $28

ELENA GIANINI BELOTTI. *The Bitter Taste of Strangers Bread*. Vol 73. Fiction. $24

PINO APRILE. *Terroni*. Vol 72. Italian Studies. $20

EMANUEL DI PASQUALE. *Harvest*. Vol 71. Poetry. $10

ROBERT ZWEIG. *Return to Naples*. Vol 70. Memoir. $16

AIROS & CAPPELLI. *Guido*. Vol 69. Italian/American Studies. $12

FRED GARDAPHÉ. *Moustache Pete is Dead! Long Live Moustache Pete!*. Vol 67. Literature/Oral History. $12

PAOLO RUFFILLI. *Dark Room/Camera oscura*. Vol 66. Poetry. $11

HELEN BAROLINI. *Crossing the Alps*. Vol 65. Fiction. $14

COSMO FERRARA. *Profiles of Italian Americans*. Vol 64. Italian Americana. $16

GIL FAGIANI. *Chianti in Connecticut*. Vol 63. Poetry. $10

BASSETTI & D'ACQUINO. *Italic Lessons*. Vol 62. Italian/American Studies. $10

CAVALIERI & PASCARELLI, Eds. *The Poet's Cookbook*. Vol 61. Poetry/Recipes. $12

EMANUEL DI PASQUALE. *Siciliana*. Vol 60. Poetry. $8

NATALIA COSTA, Ed. *Bufalini*. Vol 59. Poetry. $18.

RICHARD VETERE. *Baroque*. Vol 58. Fiction. $18.

LEWIS TURCO. *La Famiglia/The Family*. Vol 57. Memoir. $15

NICK JAMES MILETI. *The Unscrupulous*. Vol 56. Humanities. $20

BASSETTI. ACCOLLA. D'AQUINO. *Italici: An Encounter with Piero Bassetti.* Vol 55. Italian Studies. $8

GIOSE RIMANELLI. *The Three-legged One.* Vol 54. Fiction. $15

CHARLES KLOPP. *Bele Antiche Stòrie.* Vol 53. Criticism. $25

JOSEPH RICAPITO. *Second Wave.* Vol 52. Poetry. $12

GARY MORMINO. *Italians in Florida.* Vol 51. History. $15

GIANFRANCO ANGELUCCI. *Federico F.* Vol 50. Fiction. $15

ANTHONY VALERIO. *The Little Sailor.* Vol 49. Memoir. $9

ROSS TALARICO. *The Reptilian Interludes.* Vol 48. Poetry. $15

RACHEL GUIDO DE VRIES. *Teeny Tiny Tino's Fishing Story.* Vol 47. Children's Literature. $6

EMANUEL DI PASQUALE. *Writing Anew.* Vol 46. Poetry. $15

MARIA FAMÀ. *Looking For Cover.* Vol 45. Poetry. $12

ANTHONY VALERIO. *Toni Cade Bambara's One Sicilian Night.* Vol 44. Poetry. $10

EMANUEL CARNEVALI. *Furnished Rooms.* Vol 43. Poetry. $14

BRENT ADKINS. et al., Ed. *Shifting Borders. Negotiating Places.* Vol 42. Conference. $18

GEORGE GUIDA. *Low Italian.* Vol 41. Poetry. $11

GARDAPHÈ, GIORDANO, TAMBURRI. *Introducing Italian Americana.* Vol 40. Italian/American Studies. $10

DANIELA GIOSEFFI. *Blood Autumn/Autunno di sangue.* Vol 39. Poetry. $15/$25

FRED MISURELLA. *Lies to Live By.* Vol 38. Stories. $15

STEVEN BELLUSCIO. *Constructing a Bibliography.* Vol 37. Italian Americana. $15

ANTHONY JULIAN TAMBURRI, Ed. *Italian Cultural Studies 2002.* Vol 36. Essays. $18

BEA TUSIANI. *con amore.* Vol 35. Memoir. $19

FLAVIA BRIZIO-SKOV, Ed. *Reconstructing Societies in the Aftermath of War.* Vol 34. History. $30

TAMBURRI. et al., Eds. *Italian Cultural Studies 2001.* Vol 33. Essays. $18

ELIZABETH G. MESSINA, Ed. *In Our Own Voices.* Vol 32. Italian/American Studies. $25

STANISLAO G. PUGLIESE. *Desperate Inscriptions.* Vol 31. History. $12

HOSTERT & TAMBURRI, Eds. *Screening Ethnicity.* Vol 30. Italian/American Culture. $25

G. PARATI & B. LAWTON, Eds. *Italian Cultural Studies.* Vol 29. Essays. $18

HELEN BAROLINI. *More Italian Hours.* Vol 28. Fiction. $16

FRANCO NASI, Ed. *Intorno alla Via Emilia.* Vol 27. Culture. $16

ARTHUR L. CLEMENTS. *The Book of Madness & Love.* Vol 26. Poetry. $10

JOHN CASEY, et al. *Imagining Humanity.* Vol 25. Interdisciplinary Studies. $18

ROBERT LIMA. *Sardinia/Sardegna.* Vol 24. Poetry. $10

DANIELA GIOSEFFI. *Going On.* Vol 23. Poetry. $10

ROSS TALARICO. *The Journey Home.* Vol 22. Poetry. $12

EMANUEL DI PASQUALE. *The Silver Lake Love Poems.* Vol 21. Poetry. $7

JOSEPH TUSIANI. *Ethnicity.* Vol 20. Poetry. $12

JENNIFER LAGIER. *Second Class Citizen.* Vol 19. Poetry. $8